Mighty Magnets

This course was written by
Naturally Curious Expert
Michele Caton

Michele Caton is an immunologist. Right now,
she is curious about the life of plants and how the
galaxies were formed.

Copyright © 2014 by Be Naturally Curious, LLC.

All rights reserved. No part of this publication may be reproduced, distributed,
or transmitted in any form or by any means, including photocopying, recording, or other
electronic or mechanical methods, without the prior written permission of the publisher.

Printed by CreateSpace

ISBN 978-1-942403-02-9

www.benaturallycurious.com

Many activities in this book make use of printed materials. If you prefer not to cut them directly from this book, please visit the URL listed below and enter the code for a supplemental PDF containing all printable materials.

URL: www.benaturallycurious.com/magnets-printables/

password: **ferromagnetic**

Table of Contents

Required materials: Strong horseshoe magnet (roughly 4 inches in length), medium-sized bar magnet (roughly 2.5 inches in length), small, bendable refrigerator magnet, compass, large shallow dish (such as a pie pan), plastic cap (from a milk or water jug), long sewing needle (check that it is ferromagnetic), at least 6 paper clips (jumbo size works best), Scotch tape, ruler or tape measure, scissors, pencil, blank paper for drawing, small plastic bag

Magnets

Have you ever decorated your refrigerator with magnets? Maybe you used alphabet magnets to spell your name, or you collected magnets from different places you have visited. Did you ever wonder how those magnets were able to stick to the refrigerator? Today, we are going to explore the world of MAGNETISM and find out about a cool invisible force that is happening all around us.

Let's go over to a refrigerator and think about how our magnet behaves near it.

What do you feel when you hold your magnet close to the refrigerator? Do you feel a "tug"?

Once you let go of the magnet, what happens? Does it fall from the refrigerator, or does it stick?

What is the force that causes the magnet to stick to the refrigerator? It is called MAGNETISM, and it happens when a special object called a MAGNET attracts certain materials (usually metal, like a refrigerator).

Can you see magnetism happening? No, but that is because it involves very small particles that are too tiny to see with our eyes. To think about magnetism, we must pay attention to ATOMS, which are the building blocks of all objects (even refrigerator magnets). Atoms are made up of ELECTRONS circling around a NUCLEUS.

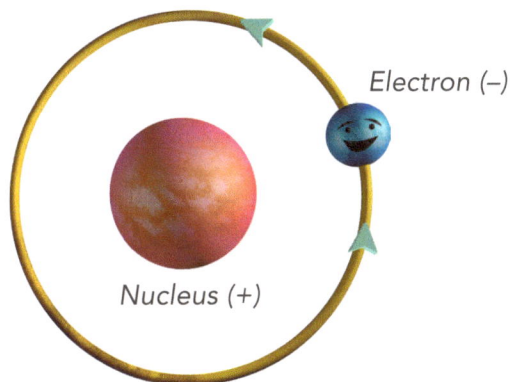

> **M**agnetism is a force that happens when objects called magnets attract certain materials.

> **I**n an atom, electrons circle around a nucleus.

Electron (–)

Nucleus (+)

HYDROGEN ATOM

© Be Naturally Curious, LLC. All rights reserved.

Although atoms have only one nucleus, they can have different numbers of electrons. For example, the oxygen atoms that you breathe each contain 8 electrons, while the iron atoms in your refrigerator magnet each have 26 electrons. Groups of atoms can join up in different combinations to make **MOLECULES**, which make up all kinds of objects, from the water you drink to the chair in which you're sitting.

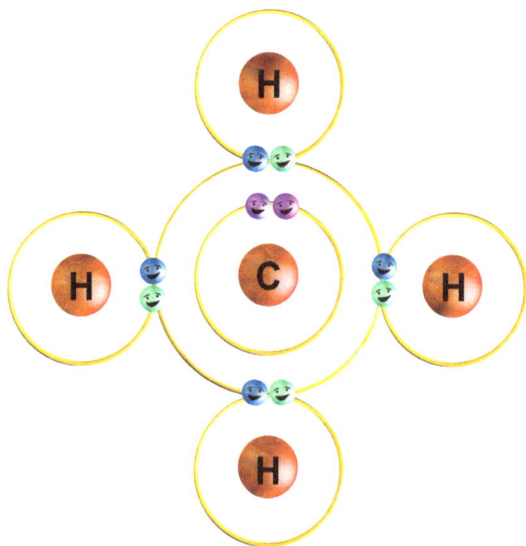

METHANE MOLECULE

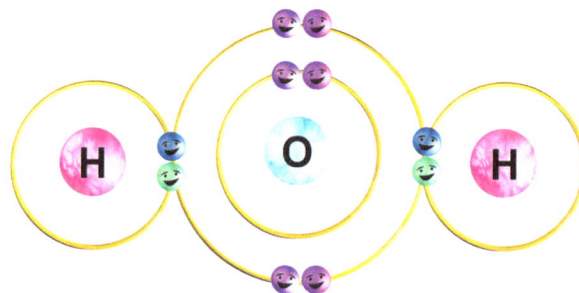

WATER MOLECULE

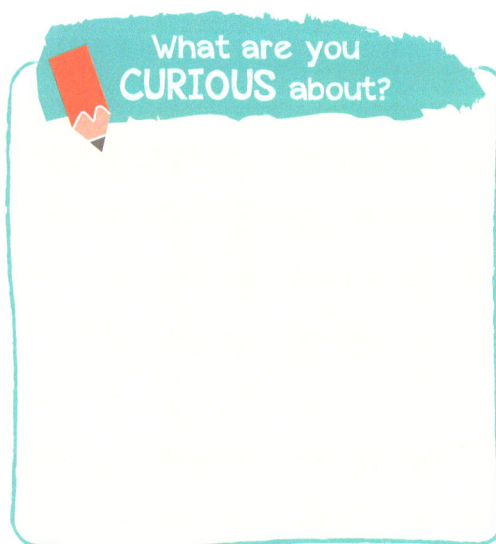

What are you CURIOUS about?

© Be Naturally Curious, LLC. All rights reserved.

Now that we know about electrons, let's see what they are doing in their atoms.

It turns out that electrons actually MOVE! Electrons whiz around the nucleus very quickly, and their motion creates tiny amounts of energy. Electrons are also very friendly and like to swing around the nucleus in pairs. However, the different electron pairs in each atom swing around in OPPOSITE directions, and then something interesting happens to their energies—they cancel each other out!

Imagine if you were swimming around the edge of a round swimming pool and trying to make a whirlpool. Now imagine if your friend also tried to make a whirlpool next to you but swam in the opposite direction. Instead of making a whirlpool, the water would probably stand still because its energy in either direction would be canceled out. The same thing happens in atoms with paired electrons.

Some atoms, however, have UNPAIRED ELECTRONS that travel alone. Since they have no other electrons to bother them, they are able to make tiny amounts of energy in one direction. That energy is called a MAGNETIC MOMENT—a tiny mini-magnet!

When electrons move as pairs, they move in different directions and they cancel out each others' energy.

When electrons are unpaired, their movement releases energy called a *magnetic moment*. This is a mini-magnet!

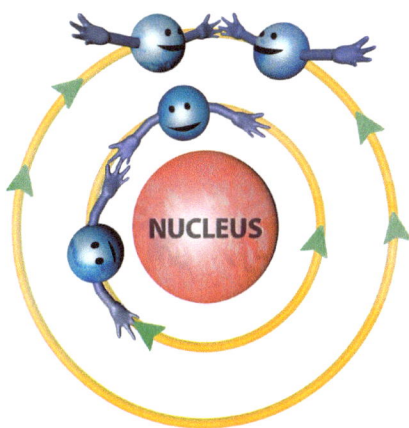

PAIRED ELECTRONS *have energies moving in opposite directions—the energies cancel each other out.*

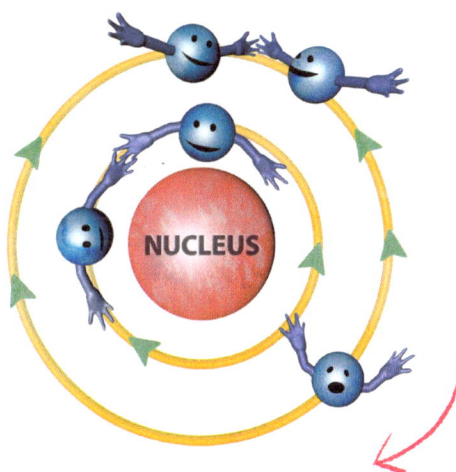

UNPAIRED ELECTRONS *have no partners to cancel out their energies— that causes them to make energy in a certain direction—a magnetic moment.*

© Be Naturally Curious, LLC. All rights reserved.

Some atoms are what we call metals, and these types of atoms often have unpaired electrons. You might think that most metals should act like magnets because their unpaired electrons would make small magnetic moments, but they don't. Why is that?

Only some metals can become magnets.

Well, it all comes down to cooperation. Remember we said that atoms come together to form molecules and finally objects? For example, in a block of metal that you hold, like a piece of gold, there are millions of atoms! What do you think would happen if all the atoms in a block of metal had magnetic moments that pointed in different directions? Most likely, you'd have a crazy, jumbled mess! In order for an object to act like a magnet, all of its magnetic moments in all of its atoms must point in the same direction, like this:

Unmagnetized Molecules

Magnetic moments point in different directions.

Magnetized Molecules

Magnetic moments point in the same direction.

Now, *that's* what makes a magnet! But how do we convince all of the magnetic moments to point in the same direction? There are a couple of ways. We can change the temperature of the object, run electricity through it, or put it near another magnet. Wait! A magnet can be made from another magnet? Yes, magnetism is contagious!

Magnets are mostly made from only a few metals (types of atoms): iron, nickel, and cobalt. These metals are special because after they are altered to become magnetic, they can stay that way permanently—that is, their electrons keep moving all in the same direction! Other metals go back to normal after the electricity is removed or after they have been away from another magnet for a while. "Going back to normal" means that their electrons go back to moving in all directions.

Most magnets are made of iron, nickel, or cobalt.

© Be Naturally Curious, LLC. All rights reserved.

So, we know that a magnet is an object whose unpaired electrons make energy when they move in the same direction. Why does that energy cause a magnet to stick to a refrigerator? Well, when the electron energies (the magnetic moments) all march together, they create a strong force that flows around the magnet. That force is called the MAGNETIC FIELD. The magnetic field flows out of one end of the magnet into the opposite end. (We call those ends POLES.) Each magnet has a north pole and a south pole, just as Earth does.

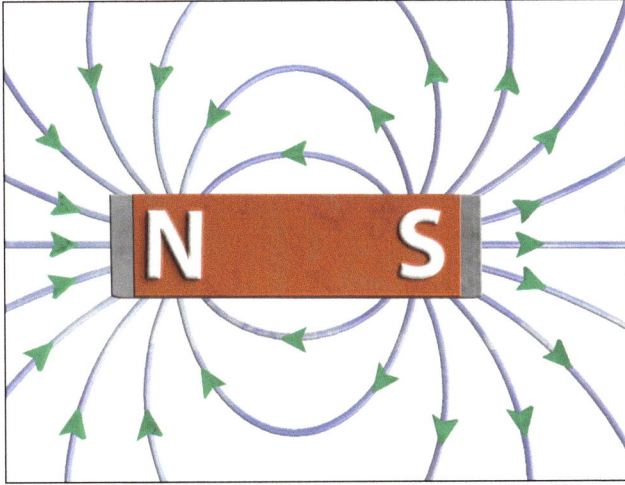

Bar magnet with magnetic field lines

A *magnetic field* is a force that flows from one end of the magnet around to the other end of the magnet.

The magnetic field tugs at (or ATTRACTS) atoms containing a lot of unpaired electrons and convinces those electrons to march together, too.

The magnetic field will tug at any unpaired electrons and make them march along in the same direction as the field.

© Be Naturally Curious, LLC. All rights reserved.

As a result, the force of magnetism causes the two objects to stick together. The atoms that are attracted to magnets are called FERROMAGNETIC. The neat part is that ferromagnetic atoms are iron, nickel, and cobalt—the same atoms that make magnets in the first place!

Atoms that are attracted to magnets are called *ferromagnetic*.

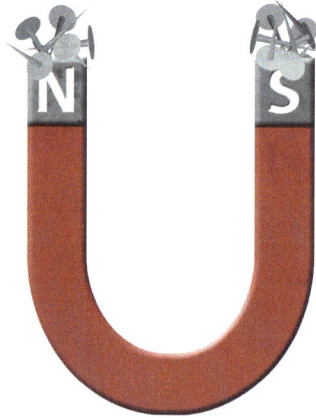

Nails containing iron are
FERROMAGNETIC.

Why are magnets important? What can they do? Well, magnets work in many appliances and electronics around your house. One of the most important examples is your computer's hard drive, where its memory is stored. Did you ever wonder how your computer remembers so many things? Inside the hard drive is a thin film that is divided into tiny sections that get magnetized when you press "Save." The direction of the electrons' magnetic moments in each section makes a code that your computer can read back to you. The film stays magnetized even when you turn off the computer, so the code never goes away.

Magnets are also used to help doctors figure out if a patient has an injury or a disease. A machine that uses MRI (magnetic resonance imaging) has an extremely strong magnet that peeks inside the human body. The MRI machine magnetizes atoms in bones and organs for a very short time. As the atoms snap back to normal, they let go of a tiny amount of energy. The MRI machine can "see" the energies from all of the atoms and form a picture of the inside of the body. I bet you didn't know that your body could be magnetized!

What are you
CURIOUS about?

© Be Naturally Curious, LLC. All rights reserved.

Can you guess what the biggest magnet is? Here's a hint: You're standing on it. That's right—Earth! Our planet is actually a giant magnet! Earth's core is filled with molten iron and nickel. As the superhot metals move, they create a magnetic field that flows out of the South Magnetic Pole and into the North Magnetic Pole to surround the planet. (The magnetic poles aren't exactly the same as the geographic North and South Poles. The magnetic poles are close to the geographic poles, but their positions change over time.)

Did you know that all of the planets in our solar system, except Venus and Mars, have their own magnetic fields?

Earth's magnetic field is very important to us because it blocks particles coming from the Sun that can be harmful to living things. We humans also depend on the planet's magnetic field to help us find where we're going. A compass has an iron or nickel needle that is magnetized by Earth's field and points in the direction of the North Magnetic Pole. Once a traveler has located the direction of north, he or she can easily find south, east, and west. Some animals, like birds and turtles, have built-in compasses that feel the magnetic field, which helps them know where to go when they migrate.

Wow, magnetism is an amazing force that really is all around us! Now that we understand how it works, let's go explore it!

The biggest magnet around is the earth itself!

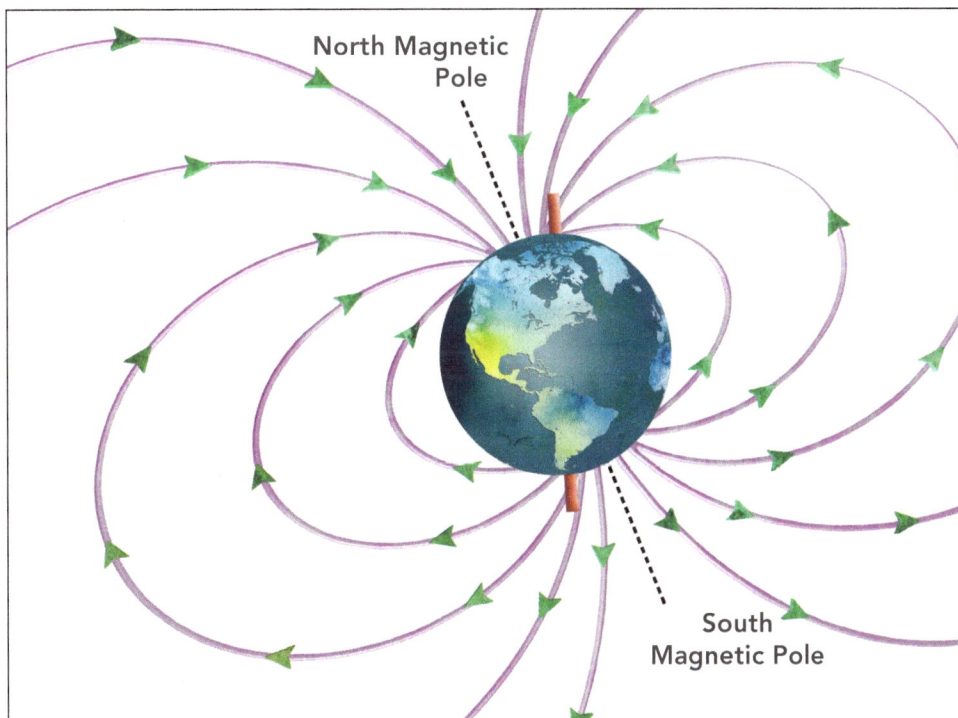

North Magnetic Pole

South Magnetic Pole

© Be Naturally Curious, LLC. All rights reserved.

Ferromagnetic Scavenger Hunt

INSTRUCTIONS

Do you remember what we call materials that are attracted to magnets? That's right, they are FERROMAGNETIC! These materials have unpaired electrons that are attracted to a magnetic field. Your quest today is to earn cool magnet badges by finding as many ferromagnetic objects as you can.

To start the hunt, take your magnet and test it on objects around your house. On the scavenger hunt chart (pages 14–15), write down each object that you tested and whether or not it is ferromagnetic. Count up your ferromagnetic objects at the end of the hunt to see which badges you earned. If you found ten ferromagnetic objects, you're a Magnet Rock Star. If you found fifteen objects, you're a Magnet Wizard! Make sure to cut out your badge on page 26.

Did you find a lot of objects that are attracted to your magnet? How are these objects similar? What are they made of? Are they hard or soft? Were you surprised that any of them were ferromagnetic? Now examine the objects that are *not* attracted to your magnet. Why do you think they are not ferromagnetic?

Challenge

Do the same scavenger hunt around the outside of your house or on your block. I bet you'll be surprised by how many ferromagnetic objects you'll find!

> ### MATERIALS
> - two or more players
> - one strong horseshoe magnet (roughly 4 inches in length) for each player
> - pencil

What are you CURIOUS about?

© Be Naturally Curious, LLC. All rights reserved.

Ferromagnetic Scavenger Hunt

PARENTS' GUIDE

A large horseshoe magnet will work best for this activity. These magnets are available online from most educational toy vendors.

Warning: Some electronics can be damaged by magnetic fields! Make sure children avoid placing their magnet near TVs, stereo equipment, computers, and cell phones. Also, credit cards store information in their magnetic strips, so have kids keep their magnet away from wallets to avoid erasing any credit cards.

Objects that are likely to be ferromagnetic include refrigerators and ovens, cast-iron pipes and radiators (found in older buildings and houses), cars, paper clips, some doorknobs, fireplace gratings, and tools.

Objects that are metal but not ferromagnetic include stainless steel appliances, copper pipes, coins, and mirrors.

© Be Naturally Curious, LLC. All rights reserved.

Scavenger Hunt Chart

ACTIVITY 1

	Name of Object	What is it made from (metal, plastic, etc.)?	Is it ferromagnetic?	
			Yes	No
1				
2				
3				
4				
5				
6				
7				
8				
9				

© Be Naturally Curious, LLC. All rights reserved.

Scavenger Hunt Chart

ACTIVITY 1

	Name of Object	What is it made from (metal, plastic, etc.)?	Is it ferromagnetic?	
			Yes	No
10				
11				
12				
13				
14				
15				
16				
17				
18				

© Be Naturally Curious, LLC. All rights reserved.

ACTIVITY
2

Investigating Your Magnets!

INSTRUCTIONS

Now that we've found some ferromagnetic objects, let's look a bit more closely at the magnetic field that is grabbing them! Magnets create a magnetic field, and although the field is invisible, we can learn a lot about it by testing it in different ways.

STRENGTH!

Do some magnets attract objects better than other magnets? Do all magnetic fields have the same strength? Well, let's find out! Place six paper clips side by side on a table. Now touch one magnet to the center of the row and count how many paper clips stick to the magnet. To get the best answer, test your magnet three times and write down the average number of paper clips picked up. Make sure to look at the feature box on page 18 to learn how to calculate an average!

MATERIALS

- Three different magnets of different sizes*
- paper clips (jumbo size works best)
- Scotch tape
- ruler or tape measure
- pen or pencil

Line up your six paper clips in a straight row.

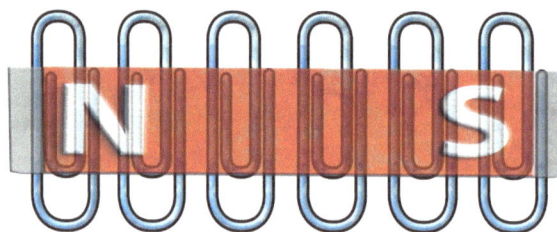

Place your magnet flat on top of the middle of the row (shaded box).

Now test all three of your magnets. Does one magnet pick up more paper clips than the others? That means its magnetic field is stronger than those of the other magnets. Use your test numbers to see which magnet is the strongest and which is the weakest.

_____

*This activity works best when magnets of significantly different strengths are used. We recommend using a small, bendable refrigerator magnet, a medium-sized bar magnet (roughly 2.5 inches in length), and a large horseshoe magnet (roughly 4 inches in length). Educational toy vendors sell multipacks of different magnet types, and Amazon.com has a nice selection under the category "Learning/Educational Toys."

© Be Naturally Curious, LLC. All rights reserved.

ACTIVITY
2

Investigating Your Magnets!

INSTRUCTIONS (continued)

Write down how many paper clips your magnet picked up each time and find the average.

	Test 1	Test 2	Test 3	Average

Magnet 1:   _____ + _____ + _____ ÷ 3 = _____

Magnet 2:   _____ + _____ + _____ ÷ 3 = _____

Magnet 3:   _____ + _____ + _____ ÷ 3 = _____

For each magnet, color in the number of blocks that matches the average number of paper clips picked up.

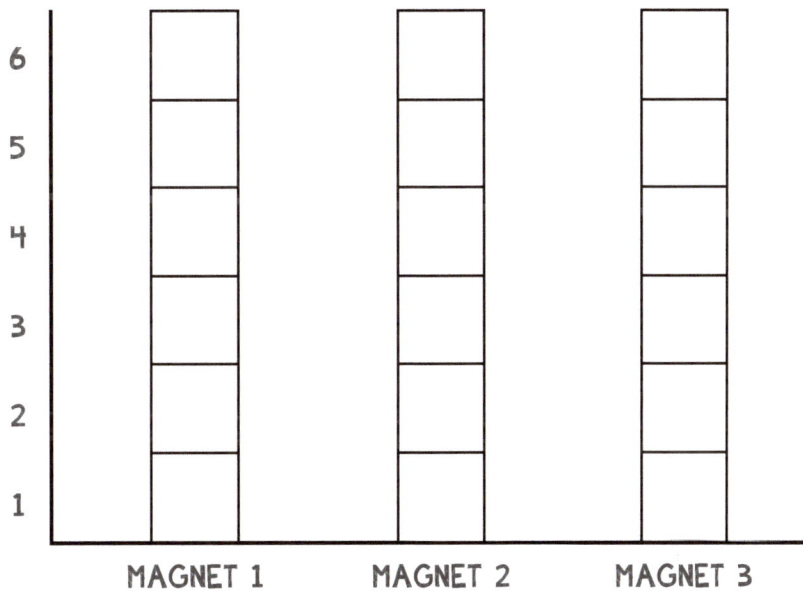

WHICH MAGNET PICKED UP THE MOST PAPER CLIPS?

_____

© Be Naturally Curious, LLC. All rights reserved.

Investigating Your Magnets!

INSTRUCTIONS (continued)

Why are some magnets stronger than others? Well, some special magnets are made of rare metals that create very strong magnetic fields. Since most household magnets are made of iron and nickel, the size of the magnet usually determines how strong it is. Did your largest magnet turn out to be the strongest magnet?

How to Calculate an Average

What if you wanted to know how long it usually takes you to brush your teeth in the morning? You could set a timer each day and write down the number of seconds it takes. But what if you were running late on one of the days and rushed through it? Or what if you were very sleepy another day and brushed slowly? Which time is more accurate? Scientists deal with this problem by repeating their measurements and recording the average number.

The Average	=	(all of the measurements added up)	÷	the number of measurements

If you added up 30 teeth-brushing times and divided by 30, you would get an answer closest to how long it usually takes you each morning.

MATERIAL!

Magnets are made of a special material (usually a metal) that creates the magnetic field. If an object made of a different material comes between your magnet and the paper clips, will the magnet still attract them? Let's find out!

Use your strongest horseshoe magnet for this test. Place six paper clips in a row and count how many stick to your magnet. Do the test three times and find the average number of paper clips picked up. Now completely cover the magnetic part of your magnet with Scotch tape and try attracting the paper clips again. Does your magnet still pick them up? Why or why not?

© Be Naturally Curious, LLC. All rights reserved.

© Be Naturally Curious, LLC. All rights reserved.

ACTIVITY
2

Investigating Your Magnets!

INSTRUCTIONS (continued)

Write down how many paper clips your magnet picked up each time and find the average.

	Test 1	Test 2	Test 3	Average
Without tape:	_____	+ _____	+ _____	÷ 3 = _____
With tape:	_____	+ _____	+ _____	÷ 3 = _____

Color in the number of boxes that matches the average number of paper clips picked up.

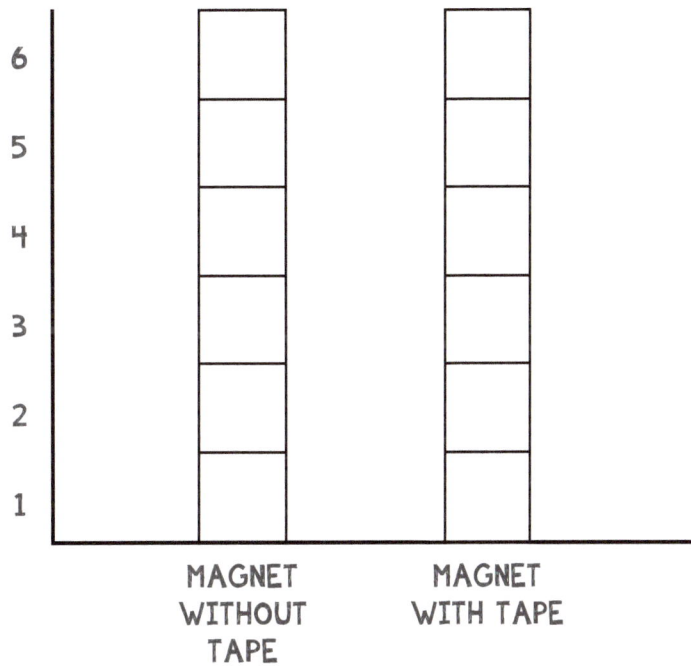

MAGNET WITHOUT TAPE   MAGNET WITH TAPE

DO YOU SEE A DIFFERENCE IN YOUR MAGNET'S STRENGTH
WHEN A PIECE OF TAPE IS COVERING IT?

_____

19

ACTIVITY
2

Investigating Your Magnets!

INSTRUCTIONS (continued)

Your magnet probably still works fine when covered in tape. The tape is made of a plastic material that is not magnetic and therefore does not interfere with the magnetic field of your magnet. But what if you flip your horseshoe magnet over so the magnetic side is facing up? Now test it on your paper clips. Does your magnet work?

Your magnet probably doesn't work anymore! Why not? A piece of tape allows the magnetic field through, but the material on the flip side of your magnet doesn't. What's going on? The answer might have to do with…

DISTANCE!

A magnet must be close to its targets in order to attract them. The piece of tape is very thin and doesn't really change the distance between the magnet and the paper clips. The flip side of the magnet is thicker and creates enough distance between the magnet and the paper clips to prevent them from feeling the magnetic field.

So, how close must the magnet be to attract the paper clips? You can measure the distance with a ruler or tape measure. Use your strongest magnet first. Line up your paper clips on the table and hold the ruler perpendicular to (standing straight up on) the table. You'll have to get eye level with the table and ruler, and watch closely. Now, slowly lower your magnet to the paper clips and note on your ruler the distance at which the paper clips "jump" to the magnet. You can try the test on all three of your magnets (take the average of three times). Is the distance the same for all three? Does the distance change according to the strength of the magnet?

Write down at what distance (in centimeters) your magnet was from the paper clips when they "jumped" to it and find the average.

	Test 1	Test 2	Test 3	Average
Magnet 1:	_____ +	_____ +	_____ ÷	3 = _____
Magnet 2:	_____ +	_____ +	_____ ÷	3 = _____
Magnet 3:	_____ +	_____ +	_____ ÷	3 = _____

© Be Naturally Curious, LLC. All rights reserved.

© Be Naturally Curious, LLC. All rights reserved.

ACTIVITY
2

Investigating Your Magnets!

INSTRUCTIONS (continued)

Color in the number of blocks that match the reading on your tape measure when the paper clips jump to the magnet.

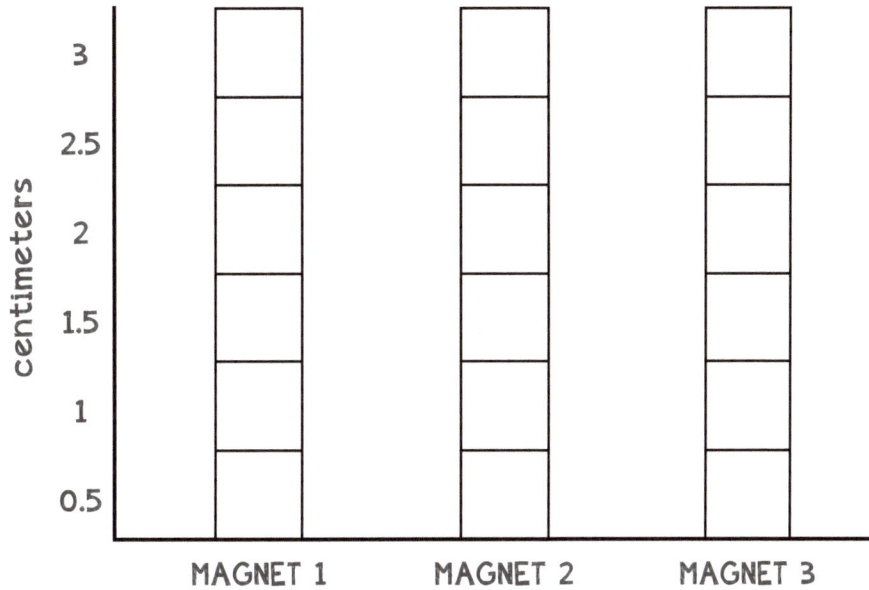

CAN SOME OF YOUR MAGNETS PICK UP PAPER CLIPS FROM FARTHER AWAY THAN OTHER MAGNETS?

_____

_____

Even though a magnetic field is invisible, you have tested it enough to learn a lot about it! What else would you like to know about your magnets, and what tests should you do to find the answers?

_____

_____

_____

_____

ACTIVITY 3

"Give Me a Magnetic Moment" Card Game

INSTRUCTIONS

Most electrons like to march around their atoms in pairs, but some unpaired electrons swing around by themselves. The unpaired electrons make a type of energy called a magnetic moment. When all the magnetic moments of a block of metal move the same way, that metal becomes a magnet.

In this game, your mission is to be the first player to make the magnetic moments of all four unpaired iron electrons point in the same direction. Here's how to play:

MATERIALS

- 3 or more players
- game board
- game cards
- scissors
- small plastic bag

1. Each player gets a game board (pages 29 and 31). If you have more than two players, print additional copies of the game board as needed.

2. Cut out the cards on page 33 and put them in a small plastic bag.

3. Players take turns drawing a card from the bag. Players are trying to collect arrow cards, such that all their arrows point the same direction around the circle (either clockwise or counter clockwise). Red dots on arrow cards should always be "up." If a player draws an arrow he or she can use, it can be placed on the game board in the correct spot.

4. Play continues as players take turns drawing cards. If a player draws a card he or she cannot use, it should be returned to the bag and it is the next player's turn.

    If a player draws a lightning bolt card, he or she can place it on top of the arrow of an opponent (if no opponent has an arrow, the lightning bolt card should be returned to the bag.)

    A player with a lightning bolt on his or her arrow must draw a magnet rescue card to remove the lightning bolt and reveal the arrow again. Players are allowed to keep any unneeded magnet rescue cards they draw for later use.

5. Keep playing until one player's electrons are all "moving" in the same direction. That means that from each player's perspective, he or she will have one arrow pointing up (on the right or left side of the board), one arrow pointing down (on the right or left side of the board), one arrow pointing to the left (on the top or bottom of the board), and one arrow pointing to the right (on the top or bottom of the board). To complete your board, all the arrows must be pointing around the circle in the same direction. When you've done this yell "Magnet!"

© Be Naturally Curious, LLC. All rights reserved.

© Be Naturally Curious, LLC. All rights reserved.

ACTIVITY 4

Let Your Magnet Show the Way!

INSTRUCTIONS

People have been using magnets to find their way around the world for hundreds of years. A magnet can detect Earth's magnetic field and point in the direction of north. We call that magnet a compass. Long ago, when an explorer arrived in an unfamiliar land, he would use a compass to draw a map so future travelers could find their way to the same place. In modern times, we still use compasses to find our way. We take them hiking, they can be found on our car's dashboard, and small boats still use them for navigating the seas. Today, we will use what we've learned about magnets to build our own compass and draw a map!

First, we'll build our compass:

1. Fill your dish with water and float the jug cap flat side down in the center of the water.

2. Magnetize your sewing needle by rubbing the needle in **one direction** across your magnet from the north pole to the south pole 70 times. Always move the needle from the north pole towards the south pole and make sure the large, flat end of the needle (the eye) goes first. The needle is made of ferromagnetic nickel and will become magnetized by the magnetic field of the magnet. So, your needle is now a magnet! (Tip: You can see your compass more easily if you mark the flat side of the needle with bright nail polish before magnetizing it.)

3. Gently balance the needle across the top of the jug cap. Make sure the cap floats near the center.

4. The large, flat end of the needle (the eye) will swing around. Note where it points when it finally stops. It will stop in the direction of north. You can check it with another compass to make sure it works correctly.

MATERIALS

- large shallow dish (a pie plate works well)
- plastic milk or water jug cap
- long sewing needle (test that it is ferromagnetic first!)
- bar magnet (roughly 2.5 inches in length)
- compass to check your accuracy (many smartphones have a "compass" function)
- paper
- pencil

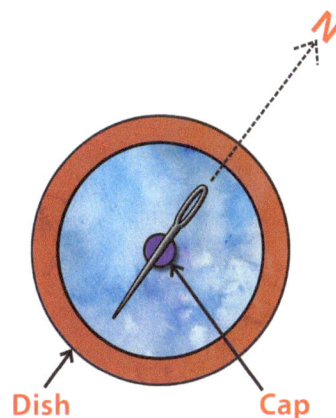

Dish   Cap

ACTIVITY
4

Let Your Magnet Show the Way!

INSTRUCTIONS (continued)

Tip: If your compass doesn't point north, try re-magnetizing your needle or using a different magnet. Also, the needle is only temporarily magnetized, so you should use your compass within a few hours of making it. Otherwise, you can magnetize it again.

Great! Now that you're a compass maker, it's time to become a cartographer (that's a mapmaker)! Use your compass, paper, and pencil to draw a map:

1. Choose the area you would like to map. Your yard or a room in your house will work well.

2. Take your compass to the area and use it to find north. Now, turn to face north.

3. Draw exactly what you see around you. If you are in your yard, draw your house, trees, other houses, and any other important objects as they appear in your yard. If you are in a room, draw the windows, door, and bigger furniture.

4. Now draw a compass rose in the corner of your map. A compass rose is a symbol on a map that shows the directions of north (N), south (S), east (E), and west (W). (It's called a rose because cartographers from long ago drew the directions very ornately to look like a flower.) Also, give your map a title so others can tell the location of your map.

Congratulations, Junior Cartographer, you've made a map!

Challenge Now that you've drawn your map, it's time to see if others can follow it. What better use for a map than finding treasure? Hide an object somewhere in your mapped area and mark its location with an "X" on your map. Now, give your map to a friend and see if he or she can find your treasure!

© Be Naturally Curious, LLC. All rights reserved.

Curiosity Connector

Here are some links to help you follow your curiosity!

- A video showing how Earth's magnetic field works:
  http://shows.howstuffworks.com/stuff-to-blow-your-mind/51304-stuff-to-blow-your-kids-mind-magnets-video.htm

- Fun magnet activities to do in your kitchen:
  http://spaghettiboxkids.com/blog/kids-science-fun-with-magnets/

- A fascinating collection of videos for adults and kids about how magnets work:
  http://science.howstuffworks.com/magnet-videos-playlist.htm

- A free online game and quiz testing the properties of magnets:
  http://www.bbc.co.uk/schools/scienceclips/ages/7_8/magnets_springs.shtml

- Explore magnetism with a kit:
  http://www.amazon.com/Thames-Kosmos-665050-Magnetic-Science/dp/B007WDGZLQ/ref=sr_1_4?s=toys-and-games&ie=UTF8&qid=1393815164&sr=1-4&keywords=magnetic+toys

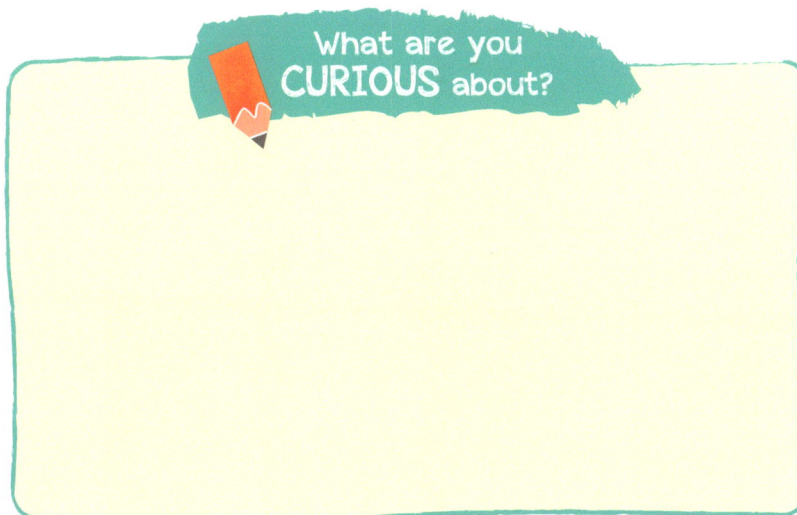

What are you CURIOUS about?

© Be Naturally Curious, LLC. All rights reserved.

Glossary

ATOMS – The building blocks of all materials. An atom contains a nucleus and electrons that circle around it.

ATTRACT – To draw something close using a physical force.

ELECTRON – The part of an atom that circles around the nucleus.

FERROMAGNETIC – Having the property of being easily attracted to a magnet.

MAGNET – An object that attracts other ferromagnetic objects with a magnetic field.

MAGNETIC FIELD – The strong force, created by electrons, that flows around a magnet.

MAGNETIC MOMENT – The tiny amount of energy made by an unpaired electron in one direction.

MAGNETISM – A force that happens when objects called magnets attract certain materials.

MOLECULES – Atoms can join together to make different kinds of molecules.

NUCLEUS – The center of an atom.

POLES – The ends of a magnet in and out of which the magnetic field flows.

UNPAIRED ELECTRON – An electron that does not have a partner to cancel out its energy.

Badges for Activity 1, page 12

© Be Naturally Curious, LLC. All rights reserved.

Tools for Your Tool Kit

Let's make the ideas you learned today part of your life tool kit. Remember to print out some blank tool kit pages and tape or glue on today's tools.

1. What part of an atom can make a magnetic field? _____

   Add an **UNPAIRED ELECTRON** to your tool kit!

2. When an unpaired electron makes a tiny bit of energy in one direction,

   that energy is called a _____ .

   Add **MAGNETIC MOMENT** to your tool kit!

3. The force that a magnet makes is called _____ .

   Add **MAGNETISM** to your tool kit!

4. When a metal like iron is attracted to a magnet, we say it is

   a _____ metal.

   Add **FERROMAGNETIC** to your tool kit!

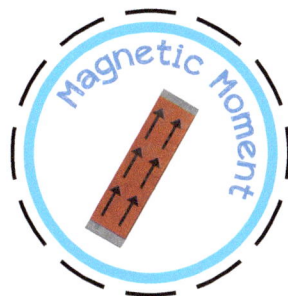

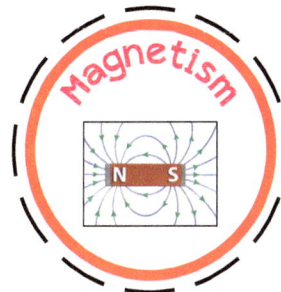

© Be Naturally Curious, LLC. All rights reserved.

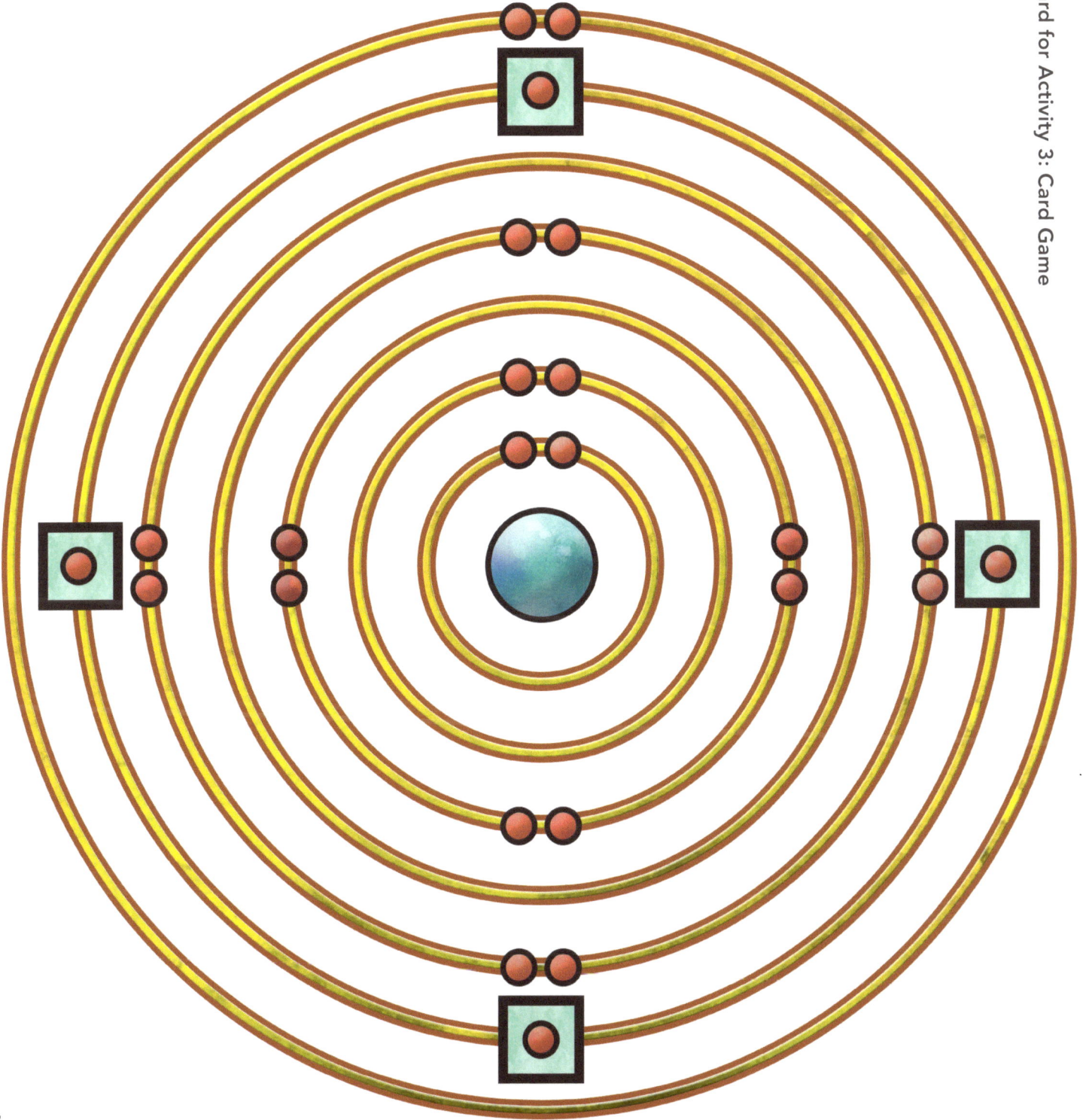

© Be Naturally Curious, LLC. All rights reserved.

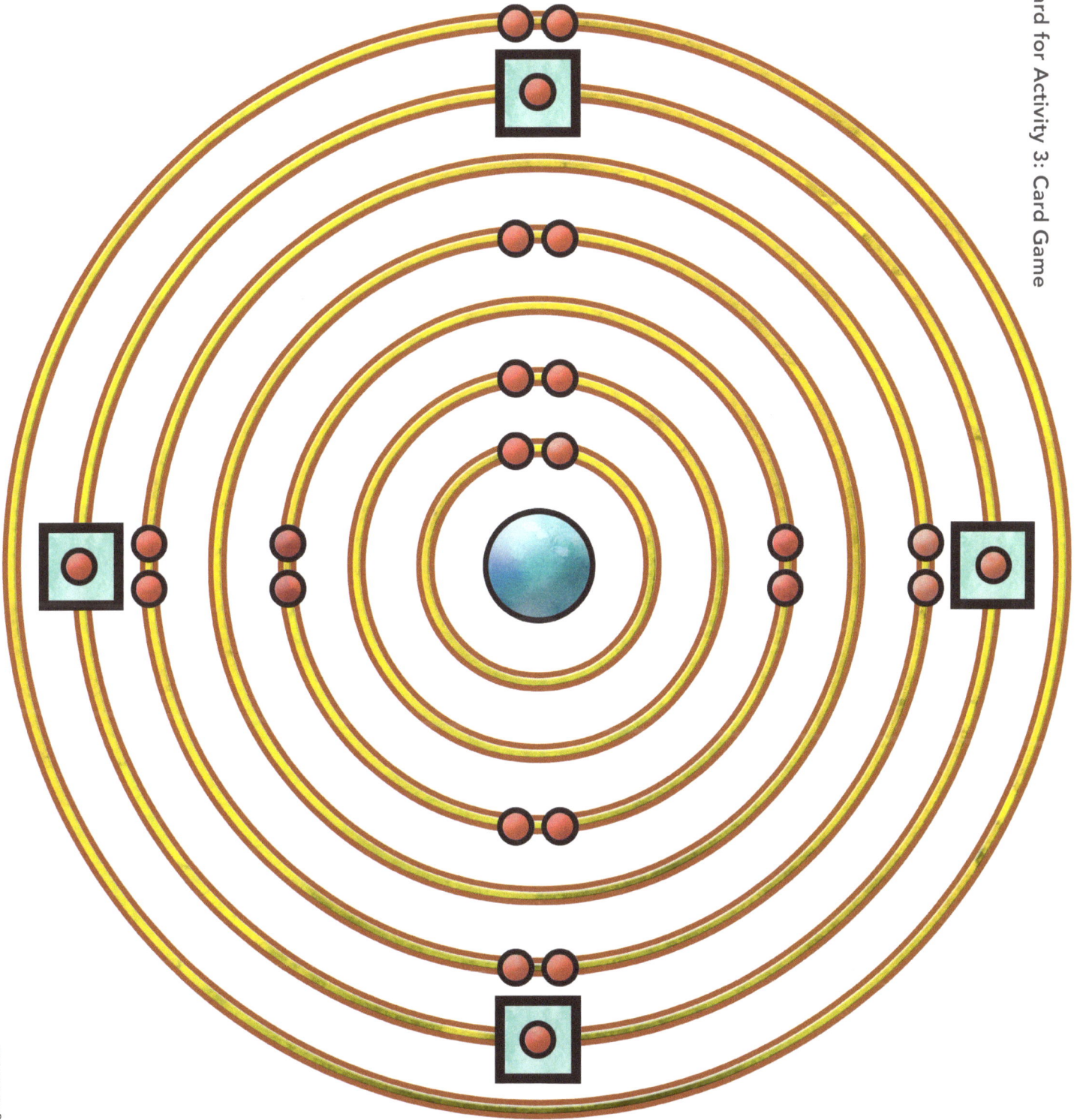

© Be Naturally Curious, LLC. All rights reserved.

Game Cards for Activity 3: Card Game

Magnet Rescue!
Magnet Rescue!
Magnet Rescue!
Magnet Rescue!
Magnet Rescue!
Magnet Rescue!
Magnet Rescue!
Magnet Rescue!
Magnet Rescue!

© Be Naturally Curious, LLC. All rights reserved.

© Be Naturally Curious, LLC. All rights reserved.

www.benaturallycurious.com

Science Tool Kit

www.ingramcontent.com/pod-product-compliance
Lightning Source LLC
LaVergne TN
LVHW072131070426
835513LV00002B/68